Atlanta Child Murders: The Insane True Crime Story

Jeffrey Patterson

TABLE OF CONTENTS

CHAPTER ONE

Edward Hope Smith, known to his friends as "Teddy," was 14-years old. He wasn't tall at 5-feet, 4-inches and he wasn't a big kid, he weighed only 125-pounds. And, like most of the victims of the Atlanta serial killer he lived in the projects. In this case, Kimberly Court on Cape Street in Atlanta.

Teddy, his girlfriend, and other friends who were classmates of his at Daniel McLaughlin Therrell High School in Atlanta, liked to roller skate at the Greenbriar Skating Rink, not too far from his home.

On this particular day, it was no different.

He skated and joked with his girlfriend. When he fell, one friend teased him unmercifully.

"You spaz. But I'm not surprised, you can barely walk without skates," joked his friend as the others laughed.

Teddy's girlfriend helped him up as he laughed and said, "I wouldn't talk if I were you. I've seen you throw a baseball."

The other kids turned their laughter toward Teddy's tormentor.

As the group laughed, Teddy and his girlfriend sprinted away and continued to transverse to the center of the rink. His friends followed.

The group seemed to enjoy themselves as they skated around the rink. They shouted out jokes and comments to each other about their skating prowess and they laughed at the quips.

When one of the kids fell, the others stopped and let him have it. Teddy could dish it out as well as take it.

"And he's down for the count," he said. And he began to count out his friend as if he were a boxer lying on the canvas after being knocked down by an opponent.

Swinging his arms he said, "One, two, three, four."

The friend scrambled back onto his skates when Teddy's knockout count reached four.

"And he's back up ladies and gentlemen and he looks like he can continue with this bout," Teddy continued.

Suddenly, the friend fell down again. And Teddy resumed the count. He reached ten before his friend could get back up on his skates.

Teddy, his girlfriend, and their other friends, including the kid who had tumbled, laughed uproariously. Teddy and his girlfriend then skated away.

The kids watched them and then one of them said, "Hey, you guys, I'm up for some French fries."

The others agree and the group skated to the edge of the rink where they climbed onto the wooden floor and clumsily went to chairs where they took off their skates. They tied their pair of skates together and threw them over their shoulders and they proceeded on to the snack bar.

Once each one of them had their snack, they all gathered at a nearby table. ate their fries and drank their milk shakes as Teddy and his girlfriend continued to skate.

After about an hour Teddy and his girlfriend joined the group at the table. They finished their snacks and were talking about school that they would have to attend the next day.

"It's after nine. My mom wants me back home by nine thirty," said Teddy to his friends. They said their goodbyes and Teddy and his girlfriend left the rink.

Teddy and his girlfriend walked together talking and laughing until they reached the intersection of Campbellton and Fairburn and then the two said their goodbyes and each walked on alone.

The date was July 21, 1979. Edward Hope Smith was never seen alive again.

Alfred James Evans was 13 years old. He was smaller than Teddy and stood only 5-feet, 4-inches and weighed only 87 pounds. He lived with his mom, Lois Evans.

A student at Drew Elementary School on East Lake Boulevard SE in Atlanta and known to his friends as Q, Evans played basketball and boxed at the Warren Memorial Boys' Club at SE Berne Street and at the East Lake Meadows Community Center. He loved watching wrestling and attended matches at the Municipal Auditorium.

On his last day, Q, of course, played basketball at the Boys' Club.

Q jumped to catch the basketball as it bounced off the backboard at the basketball court at Warren Memorial Boys' Club. He immediately started to dribble it toward the other basket at the other end of the court. As he moved he surveyed the court looking for a teammate to throw the ball to. By the time he made it up to midcourt, he spotted a teammate, threw the ball to him, and then jogged toward the basket.

The teammate dribbled through the opposition players and set up on the left side of the basket and tossed the ball all the way across the court to Q who caught it and dribbled forward a few feet, then took the shot. The ball fell through the net and Q and his team ran back toward their

basket getting ready to defend the onslaught from the opposing team.

Q confronted the player with the ball as he stopped dribbling and took a shot. Q blocked the shot, recovered the ball, hurriedly dribbled toward the basket, stopped short only feet from the basket and shot and sank the shot. The buzzer sounded to end the game.

Q and his teammates gathered to shake hands, slap fives, and congratulate each other, and then the assembly broke up.

Q left the Boys' Club and started his walk home. As he neared the intersection he heard a shout out from a friend, Randy Joe Heath, who was standing next to his car across the street.

"Hey, man. Where you heading," asked Heath.

"Home," said Q.

"Well, I can get you closer. I'm heading to the movies to meet up with a friend."

"Thanks."

Q crossed the street and joined Heath. The two got into Heath's car and they drove off.

As Heath drove the car he asked Q, "Where you coming from?"

"The Boys' Club," he said.

"What were you doing, playing B ball or boxing," asked Heath.

"Playing B ball. I don't do boxing until Saturday," Q answered.

"Hey, by the way, when's your next match?"

"Week from Saturday. I fight Johnny Davis."

"Man, you like Thomas Hearns or something."

"No, I'm more like Muhammad Ali. I float like a butterfly and sting like a bee," said Q with a smile.

"You sure are," responded Heath with a laugh. "Hey, look I'll drop you off at Glenwood. You can take a bus home from there."

"Thanks."

The car pulled up to the curb near a bus stop and Q got out. He closed the car door, waved at his friend, and walked toward the stop. That was July 25, 1979. Q was never seen alive again.

On July 28, 1979 an old woman was salvaging for cans in a sparsely wooded area on Niskey Lake Road SW in Atlanta. As she picked up a can to inspect it, she saw two lumps of something in her peripheral vision. She looked straight at the spot and discovered two dead bodies. Although the Atlanta police couldn't identify the dead children for several more weeks, they turned out to be Teddy and Q. The first two victims of a serial killer.

CHAPTER TWO

ois Evans, Q's mother, was frantic. She had not seen or heard from
Q for three days. She had called every one of his friends she could
remember, but Q wasn't with them and they didn't know where
he was. She talked to Randy Heath and he told her that he gave Q a ride to
the bus stop on Glenwood Road and then went on to meet friends to see a
movie at the Coronet Theatre on Peachtree Street.

After talking to Heath, she took a gulp, nervously picked up the phone
and dialed 911.

"911 emergency," the woman on the other end of the phone said.

Nervously, and in a whispered voice Lois responded, "My name is Lois
Evans. My boy Alfred hasn't been home for three days. I called all of his
friends and they haven't seen him since Wednesday. I talked to one friend,
Randy Heath, who said he drove my baby to a bus stop at Glenwood Road
and left him there. I'm really worried that something bad has happened to
my boy."

"How old is he, Mrs. Evans," said the woman in a calm voice.

"He's only 13."

"How tall is he and how much does he weigh?"

"He's 5-feet, 4 and weighs 87-pounds."

As Lois Evans was requesting help from the police to find her son, Teddy's mother was doing the same.

Meanwhile, a rookie detective named Danny Agan stood along with a group of other officers of the Atlanta Police Department, as they watched officers searching the wooded area on Niskey Lake Road.

It was a sizzling hot and humid day in Atlanta. Pretty much typical for the city in July. Agan had a handkerchief in his hand and was periodically using it to dab the sweat from his forehead and face. He stood at the sidelines of the crime scene watching and waiting for one of the searching officers to shout out that he had found something.

Finally, there was a response as one of the officers shouted out, "Hey, over here."

As a cluster of police including Agan quickly walked toward the officer who had called out, there was another shout from a second policeman.

"Here, too."

Agan stopped and looked at the second officer and then continued on to the first.

When he was in close proximity to the first officer he asked, "What do we have here?"

"A young black male," the officer said.

Agan looked down at the body. It was unrecognizable. The body was already decomposing and it was obvious that some animals had gotten to it. Body parts were spread out nearby.

"Any identification?"

The officer kneeled down next to the body and checked the pants pockets.

"Nothing."

"Okay, check the body and the surrounding area for evidence and get forensics working over here."

"Yes, sir."

Agan then walked toward the second officer who had found the second body as the first officer shouted for the forensic technicians.

About one hundred yards from the first body laid the other, also a young black male. It wasn't as decomposed as the first, but he too didn't have any identification.

Very little about the deaths of the first two victims of the Atlanta serial killer were covered by the media. *The Atlanta Constitution-Journal* tucked a story about the discovery of two unidentified black children's bodies deep into the A section of an August 1979 edition. But, while most of the population of the city were unaware of the possibility that there was a serial killer stalking black children, fear gripped the affected community. They were unaware that the police had found the bodies because they didn't know the name of the victims. And, being a southern city in the United States in the 1970s, the life and death of black children was not a major issue. After all, the citizens of the city woke up every day and were hearing or reading about murders of blacks to a point where it wasn't considered a major thing unless you were a relative or friend of the victim. After all, Atlanta was considered to be the murder capital of the United States.

Students and teachers were wondering about the whereabouts of Teddy Smith. The principal of the school called Teddy's mother, but all he could discover was that he was missing.

It was the same at Drew Elementary where Q went to school.

Arthur Langford Jr., community leader and director of the United Youth Adult Conference of Atlanta, a Georgia state senator, and a minister at a Baptist Church in the southwest section of Atlanta, organized searches for the missing children.

CHAPTER THREE

Tuesday, September 4, 1979 was not a special day as far as 14-year-old Milton Harvey was concerned. His mother had asked him not to go to his school, Harper High on Collier Drive NW, because she had bought the wrong shoes for him and she wanted him to accompany her when she went to the shoe store to buy him a proper pair.

In the meantime, she had sent him off with a check for $100 that she wanted him to deliver to a bank to pay a credit card bill.

He left his apartment at 1396 Nash Road NW at about 10 a.m. and climbed onto his yellow 10-speed bicycle heading off to do what his mother had requested. He never made it home.

While searching for him a week later, a neighbor of the Harveys found his bike laying next to a pine tree on Sandy Creek Road near Fulton County Airport, also known as Charlie Brown Airport.

It wasn't until November 16, 1979 that a man collecting cans in a garbage dump near the intersection of Desert Road and Redwine Road on the south side of Atlanta, stumbled upon the skeletal remains that would later be identified as Milton Harvey.

The man called 911 and the Atlanta police were summoned to the scene. Once again they searched the area and checked out the body, but they were unable to identify it. So his parents were not informed.

Just as the mothers of Edward Hope "Teddy" Smith and Alfred "Q" Evans, Milton's mother Patricia Ellis and his stepfather Roy Ellis called the boy's friends to get any information they had. None was forthcoming. They then called 911 to alert the Atlanta police of his disappearance.

The local and national media reported nothing of the incident, but rumors about someone going around and killing black children began spreading through Atlanta's African-American community like a wildfire.

Arthur Langford organized another search, but Milton Harvey wasn't found.

CHAPTER FOUR

ine year-old Yusuf Bell became the youngest victim of the Atlanta serial killer to date after he disappeared on October 21, 1979. He was going to Reese Grocery Store on McDaniel Street to buy snuff for Eula Birdsong. She was a neighbor of the Bell family at the McDaniel Glenn Housing Authority on Rawson Street SW Atlanta. Yusuf lived there with his mother, Camille, two sisters, Tonia and Marie, and a brother, Jonathan.

Yusuf was a fifth-grade student at the Dunbar Elementary School on Whitehall Terrace SW in Atlanta. He also frequented the Warren Memorial Boys' Club, where Alfred "Q" Evans went to play basketball and box.

Later the same day that Yusuf went missing, 30-year-old John Henry Tye, a school janitor, was walking through the neighborhood searching for a place to urinate in private. He entered a dilapidated building where he relieved himself. Once he finished and was on his way out, he found Yusuf's body in a crawlspace. The boy was wearing cut-off brown shorts that had a piece of masking tape stuck to them.

When Atlanta police searched the crime scene they found the snuff and a receipt from the Reese Grocery Store. Officers were sent to the store. Three black men who were at the store when Yusuf came in and bought the snuff told them that they saw the boy get into a blue car on the 300 block of Fulton Street near the store. A black female witness, who knew Yusuf's mother Camille, claimed that Yusuf's father, Camille's ex-husband John Bell, was driving the car.

Camille later told police that the female witness had a drinking problem so her claim was unreliable. John Bell was also questioned and commented that his son would be found safe. He was also given a polygraph test, which he supposedly failed.

Results of an autopsy determined that Yusuf was hit in the head twice and had been strangled.

Camille grieved for her son. But she also wanted to do something that would force the police, the politicians of Atlanta, and the media to take the murders much more seriously. She contacted mothers of previous victims and with them formed a victims' advocacy group called the Committee to Stop Children's Murders or STOP.

To get their agenda to the people of Atlanta, the group hounded the media with press conferences and arranged for interviews with reporters whenever a new victim was discovered.

The group also pressed the Atlanta Police and the Georgia Bureau of Investigation to work more aggressively in solving the murders. The media pressure was only one of their tools. They also frequently contacted law enforcement personnel who were working on the case.

The persistent campaign finally got the authorities to more aggressively pursue the killer by the summer of 1980

Fear that had started to grip the African-American community of southwest Atlanta after the disappearances of Edward Hope Smith, Alfred Evans, and Milton Harvey spiked further after the disappearance and murder of Yusuf Bell. Parents worried whenever their children were out of their sight.

When no disappearances or murders occurred from the end of 1979 through February 1980 many believed that the killings had ended.

CHAPTER FIVE

arch 4, 1980 was a typical Tuesday for 12 year-old Angel Latrice Lenair. After school at Venetian Hills Elementary she returned home at 1660 Stanton Road SW Atlanta where her mother, Venus Caroline Taylor, was preparing for work as a cocktail waitress at the Mahogany Club on Georgia Route 166 (Campbellton Road). While leaving school, a friend asked Angel over to her house to watch television. Since her friend's place was not too far from her own home, Angel decided to go home first to alert her mother of her plans.

She left home at about 4 p.m. heading for her friend's place before her mother had left for her job.

After arriving at the friend's home, the two watched *Sanford & Son* and talked about school and mutual friends. She had dinner with her friend's family and then she left to head back home at about 7:30 p.m. She never arrived home.

Her body was found six days later on March 10 in a wooded lot on Campbellton Road near the intersection with Willowbrook SW, just a few blocks from her home.

According to police, a pair of panties that didn't belong to her was stuffed into her mouth and her hands were tied together with electrical cord. She had been sexually assaulted.

The police canvassed the neighborhood questioning residents about whether they had noticed anything when the girl's body was dropped at the site. Those who were questioned included two men, one wore an electrical cord as a belt around his waist and police discovered later that he had been arrested for grabbing a child.

An autopsy found that Angel was killed by ligature strangulation.

Police believed that this crime appeared contrary to the killer's M.O. The previous victims had been male, and the evidence seemed to show that the killer was a suppressed homosexual. So the murder of a 12 year-old girl appeared to be an anomaly.

If the killer was the same man who killed Edward Hope Smith, Alfred Evans, Milton Harvey, and Yusuf Bell, he had simply taken a four-month hiatus. Whoever he was, he was still stalking black children.

Again, the killer seemed to have broken his pattern when it came to the disappearance and murder of the next victim, Jeffery Mathis.

At 11 years old, Mathis was a small kid standing only 4-feet, 8-inches and weighing just 71-pounds. A student at Joel Chandler Harris Elementary School, Mathis lived with his mother, Willie Mae Mathis, two older brothers and two sisters. After school he

often assisted customers of Kroger's Grocery Store on Cascade Avenue SW in Atlanta carry their groceries to their cars.

W. A. Williams, a barber whose shop was located at the intersection of Gordon and East Ontario told police that Mathis knocked on his shop's window on Tuesday, March 11, 1980, the day he disappeared. That's just one day after Angel Lenair's body was found at a wooded lot on Campbellton Road. This marked the first time a victim had disappeared just days after another victim had been found.

Several witnesses told police that the boy got into a blue car with a light-skinned man and a dark-skinned man on East Ontario Street. Another witness claimed that he had seen the boy in a blue Nova about two weeks after he disappeared.

Apparently after receiving a tip, FBI agents with trained dogs found the boy's body in a briar patch near Suber, Cascade, and Campbellton roads in southwest Atlanta.

While the African-American community of southwest Atlanta was panicking, the Atlanta police were bewildered. With the discovery of Mathis' body it appeared that they had no clue who the killer could be.

With the discovery of the body of the next victim, however, the police would finally find evidence that would ultimately lead to an arrest.

CHAPTER SIX

Like all of the initial victims of the Atlanta child killer, Eric Middlebrooks was just in his early teens. He was 14 years old. A student at Franklin D. Roosevelt High School, he was in the Atlanta foster home program and lived with his foster parents, Robert and Evelyn Miller, at 345 Howell Drive, apartment 11-4 in the southern region of Atlanta. His older half-brother, Kerry Middlebrooks, was a police officer. His biological mother, Charlene Middlebrooks, gave him up when he was only 4 months old. She lived in North Carolina and showed no interest in the boy. He never knew his biological father.

At about 10 p.m. on May 18, 1980, Eric answered the phone at his foster parents' home.

"Dad, phone call," he said and then put the phone receiver down next to the phone. As Robert Miller appeared in the room to take the phone call, Eric rushed out of the house, a hammer in his hand to fix his bike. His foster parents never saw him alive again.

His body was found the next day next to his bike behind the Hope-U-Like-It bar at 247 Flat Shoal Road.

Just a few weeks before he disappeared, Eric had testified against three juveniles who were accused of robbery.

Rookie detective Danny Agan, who was involved in the crime scene investigation for Edward Hope "Teddy" Smith and Alfred "Q" Evans, had recently been paired with detective Robert Buffington, a Vietnam War veteran who had been awarded the Purple Heart.

The two were assigned to investigate.

When they arrived at the scene early in the morning of May 19, 1980, they were confronted with the body of a young black male. He was lying on his side with his athletic shoes turned up and off the ground. His pockets were turned inside out and there was a scattering of pennies, nickels, and dimes down to the street.

As Buffington examined the body, he noticed a piece of fiber caught in the rubber flap of the boy's left shoe. Buffington thought it was a carpet fiber. He guessed that the victim might have been dragged across a carpet.

He bagged the fiber along with a few more fibers he found on the boy's hair.

Buffington and Agan were back at their desks by 10 a.m. Buffington carefully placed the fibers onto pharmaceutical wraps and wrote his report

A police lieutenant had witnessed Buffington carefully wrap the fiber.

"Hey, Buff, what are you doing," asked the lieutenant.

"I'm guessing that's a carpet fiber from the killer's home," Buffington said.

At the time of the Atlanta murders, forensic science was a fairly new discipline for police departments around the country. Many in police forces were not yet aware of its importance in solving crimes. So, it was not surprising that the lieutenant was skeptical about the find.

"Tell you what," quipped the lieutenant. "Why don't you come to my house and clean out the lint out of my dryer. Then you can use it to clear every case in Atlanta."

As some police officers in the room laughed, Buffington and Agan gathered up their reports and the evidence and took a trip to the state's crime lab. Buffington asked micro-analyst Larry Peterson to take a look at the fibers.

During the next few months Peterson researched carpet fiber colors and materials whenever he had the opportunity. Over time he compiled a "book" on carpet fibers with specific information concerning stores where certain carpet styles were sold and how many of specific styles of carpets were sold in the Atlanta area.

Buffington and Agan returned to the station and began an exhaustive 36 hours trying to identify the body. They guessed that the boy was of middle-school age and looked up the names and addresses of schools in close proximity to where the body was found.

They then visited each school and reviewed the absentee reports for May 19, 1980.

When they got to Franklin D. Roosevelt High School and reviewed its absentee report, they discovered that Eric Middlebrooks was the only student who had missed school on that day as well as the day before.

They discovered later while questioning people who knew Eric that his neighbors would often request that he go to the store and buy them a pack of cigarettes or a carton of beer. He would do the errands riding his bike so that he could make some extra money.

Buffington wrote the name of Eric Middlebrooks into the station's "death book" where they listed the names of victims of homicides and suicides.

He reviewed the "book" going back a few years and compared what he found with a review of the last year. He learned that there was a significant spike in the murder of young children. He talked his findings over with Agan and the two concluded that they were dealing with a serial murderer who may be a pedophile.

Buffington then drafted a letter detailing what he had discovered and sent it to Atlanta's police major and added that he wanted him to share the information with Atlanta's Chief of Police.

The major visited Buffington at the station the next day to discuss the letter. It turned out that he was skeptical about it. At the time, it was widely believed by the country's police officers that there was no chance that a black male could be a serial killer. They believed that only white men like Ted Bundy could be serial killers.

The major told him to drop the idea and never write him a similar letter ever again. Moreover, he told Buffington not to talk to anyone about it or to do anything. He added, "We don't want a serial murderer."

Buffington realized that if the Atlanta police were to admit there was a serial killer stalking young black children in Atlanta that the whole community would be shaken and chaos would result for the political leaders of the city. Still, he thought that it was the obligation of the police force to be honest with the community about what was happening, fear and chaos be damned.

As Buffington and Agan talked about the case among themselves they realized that the victims were all known to do odd jobs for money. They trusted people, even strangers and could probably be easily manipulated by a predator.

By now the Atlanta media was extensively covering the case. Rumors spread that the Ku Klux Klan or white police officers were involved with the murders.

In order to lessen the heat from the media, the city's politicians spoke of the case releasing information on evidence found and possible leads. Police were afraid that this was tipping off the killer encouraging him to change his behavior so he wouldn't get caught.

Police were having a difficult time trying to get information from the black community because the blacks didn't trust them. Blacks who cooperated with police were considered snitches and many of their neighbors didn't trust them.

Parents hovered over their children, frantic to protect them. When possible they drove their elementary school or middle school aged children to school and picked them up and brought them home when the school day ended. If the mothers or fathers couldn't drive them, then the kids' older brothers or sisters would do it.

If their parents couldn't drive them to school and if they didn't have an older brother or sister to do it, kids would walk to and from school frightened about what was up at the next intersection or that some stranger would jump out at them from a deserted, dilapidated building.

For families who knew a child who was murdered, the fear was even greater. No matter how young the child was he or she knew that what happened to his or her friend could happen to them.

Atlanta's elected officials encouraged the community to be vigilant, to watch their kids. When the school buses arrived at a neighborhood, doors of every house on the street were open and concerned parents would watch for their own and their neighbors' kids and observe them until they were safely inside their homes.

And, as the black community of south Atlanta lived with increasing fear and foreboding, the killings continued.

CHAPTER SEVEN

F ive black children disappeared at rapid fire pace in June and July. 12-year-old Christopher Richardson was first to go missing on June 9, 1980.

A student at Hooper-Alexander Elementary School, he lived at 1495 Conway Road in East Lake Meadows with his grandparents. His father, Thomas Richardson, Jr., was in Reidsville Prison in Reidsville, Georgia serving a 15-year sentence for armed robbery and his stepfather was serving a year in jail for theft. His mother Sirlena R. Cobb was not involved in his life.

He was last seen outside a Krystal Hamburgers near the Belvedere Plaza Shopping Center on Memorial Road in DeKalb County. His plan was to go swimming at the nearby Midway Recreation Center in Midway Park.

The next to disappear was 7-year-old LaTonya Yovette Wilson, , who was a student at Jones Elementary School. Early in the morning of Sunday, June 22, 1980, She was taken from an apartment in the Hillcrest Heights Apartment Complex at 2261 NW Verbena Street in Dixie Hills, a suburb of Atlanta. She lived there with her parents, Clarence and Ella Wilson, her sister Cheryl, three brothers — Christopher, Tyress, and David -- two half-sisters and two half-brothers.

A neighbor, Gladys Durden, claimed that she saw a black man enter the apartment through a second floor window and leave the building through a back door holding LaTonya in his arms. She said that she saw the man talk to another black man in the parking lot of the apartment complex before he left.

One of the Saturday searches ordered by the City Council discovered the little girl's skeletal remains.

It was after LaTonya's disappearance that the FBI got involved in the case. The Atlanta Police and the Georgia Bureau of Investigation asked the FBI if the federal kidnapping statute had been violated.

After a review, the FBI announced that federal law did not cover any of the crimes that had occurred so far.

But John Glover, the Special Agent in Charge of the Atlanta office of the FBI, who was the first African-American to lead an FBI field office, offered to provide support.

The Atlanta office followed up on out-of-state leads and the FBI lab offered assistance as well. In addition, the office's

Behavioral Science Unit assigned an expert to create a profile of the possible killer.

As the killings continued, local politicians, the local media, and Georgia Senator Sam Nunn asked the Bureau to become officially involved.

The third child of this cluster to disappear was Aaron Darnell Wyche. He was 10 years old and lived with his mother, Linda Wyche, at 1065 Henry Thomas Drive SE, apartment 336, Atlanta.

He was last seen at Tanner's Corner Grocery at the intersection of McDonough Boulevard and Moreland Drive in southeast

Atlanta at about 4:30 p.m. A witness said that he was getting into a blue and white Chevrolet with two black men.

Another witness claimed that she saw Aaron being led by a black man who was about 6 feet tall with a moustache and goatee and weighing about 180 pounds. The witness claimed that she knew Aaron and that he acknowledged her and then continued on as if nothing was wrong. She added that Aaron and the man got into a blue 1970s late model Chevrolet that drove away.

Atlanta police said later that the boy was seen at Moreland Avenue shopping Center at 1374 Moreland Avenue SE, Atlanta.

On June 24, Aaron's body was found under a bridge over train tracks on Constitution Road near Moreland Avenue. He had died of positional asphyxiation. He also had a broken neck due to being thrown from the bridge.

The two who disappeared in July were Anthony Carter and Earl Terrell.

Anthony Bernard Carter was 9 years old. He was a student at E. R. Carter Elementary School at 80 Joseph E. Lowery Boulevard in Atlanta. He lived with his mother in a red brick apartment building at 896 W. End Avenue. He often took odd jobs around the Mall at West End at Lee Street and Ralph David Abernathy Road in west Atlanta.

He was last seen playing hide and seek with a cousin outside his home between 1:00 and 1:30 p.m. on July 6, 1980.

By this time, pressure from the public, media and victims' advocacy groups like STOP, forced then Atlanta Mayor Maynard Jackson to announce the formation of The Special Police Task Force on Missing and Murdered Children. The announcement was made during a press conference held on July 17, 1980.

From the start, the task force concentrated on disappearances that shared certain traits including the fact that young black males had vanished from public locations, that the bodies were found in desolate areas, and that the murders did not have an obvious motive. Two other murders at the time appeared to have a gang connection. The commonalities led the task force to conclude that a single killer had committed the murders.

The task force encouraged anyone who could help to come forward. A former police officer, public safety commissioner, and consultant with the Justice Department named Chet Dettlinger answered the call. He gathered several former law enforcement personnel and created a map showing from where victims were nabbed and where they were found dead. The map proved such a great tool that Dettlinger could predict where future victims would come from. When he predicted correctly on some of the cases, the police investigated him believing that he may have been the murderer. Once cleared, he and his makeshift group of consultants were invited to officially participate in the task force.

On November 6, 1980, the Attorney General of the United States, Benjamin Civiletti, announced that the Bureau would perform a preliminary investigation. On November 17, the AG announced that the FBI would launch a major case investigation.

The Bureau assigned more than 24 agents and other personnel to the investigation full time. The agents joined the Atlanta Police and the Georgia Bureau of Investigation as part of the task force to investigate the murders.

The next victim was a third-grade student at Lakewood Elementary School. Earl Lee Terrell lived with his mother, Beverly Belt, his stepfather, James Belt, and three brothers — Anthony, James, and Alexis – at 1930 Browns Mill Road SE in Atlanta. His brothers' biological father was Willie

Terrell and Earl's biological father was Bennie Yarn. His aunt, Vickie Terrell, lived next door.

On July 31, 1980, Earl went swimming at the South Bend Park Pool at 1955 Compton Drive SE in Atlanta. At about 3:30 p.m. the pool lifeguard, Olivia Hickson, kicked him out of the park.

He was seen buying freeze pops at a grocery store just one block from his home.

On October 18, 1980, Arthur Langford, Jr. and members of the United Youth Adult Conference of Atlanta discovered the skeletal remains of LaTonya Wilson in a fenced in area at the end of Verbena Street.

On January 9, 1981, A resident tipped police that he had found two dead black boys in a wooded area about 75 feet north of Redwine Street.

When the police went to the scene they found the body of Christopher Richardson and Earl Terrell. Police recovered a number of items at the scene including shotgun shells, a Penthouse and Gallery Magazine, a cigarette butt, and magnetic recording tape.

By the end of the summer it was apparent that the killer had expanded the area in which he was kidnapping and killing African-American children. Christopher Richardson lived in DeKalb County, and LaTonya Wilson lived in Dixie Hills.

It was apparent that the killer was doing what members of the Atlanta police department feared because the city's politicians were informing the public about the progress of the case.

In order to avoid capture and yet still satisfy his urge to kill, the murderer had changed his M.O.

CHAPTER EIGHT

As the investigations dragged on, the murders continued. The next victim to go missing was Clifford Jones, 12, who lived with his brothers Dwayne and Herman, a sister, Alice, and his mother, Eunice Jones, in an apartment on Lookout Avenue NW. Just prior to his disappearance on Wednesday, August 20, 1980, the 4-foot-1-inch, 87-pound boy was spending time with his grandmother, Dorothy Williams, who was visiting from Cleveland, Ohio.

He left the apartment with his cousin and went to St. James and Lookout Avenue to collect cans they would sell later.

Atlanta police, after receiving an anonymous tip, were dispatched to Hollywood Plaza Shopping Center on Hollywood Road and found Clifford's body next to a dumpster by a Laundromat.

There were bruises and cuts around the boy's mouth, his underwear was missing and he was wearing unfamiliar red and blue jogging shorts and white tennis shoes. The cause of death was asphyxiation.

Police questioned three youths in the Laundromat who claimed that they could see inside the home of the Laundromat's manager next door and saw the manager beat and strangle the boy to death and then carry the body to the dumpster.

Another witness who police referred to as "retarded," told them that he could see inside the Laundromat's manager's home next door to the Laundromat and witnessed the manager rape the boy and then strangle him with a yellow rope. He added that the manager then washed the body with soap and a rag and then re-clothed it.

Two other witnesses told police that they saw an African-American man wearing a hooded robe leave the Laundromat's manager's home carrying something in a large plastic bag that he dropped near the dumpster.

Police found a fiber that was similar to the one they found on the body of Eric Middlebrooks.

The next to disappear was Darron Glass, 11, who lived with his foster mother Fannie Mae Smith at an apartment on Memorial Drive SE. Standing only 4-foot-9 and weighing only 75 pounds, the boy attended Kirkwood Elementary School.

He had gone to an Atlanta Braves game and was last seen exiting a church bus at the corner of Glendwood Avenue SE and 2nd Avenue SE at about 5:30 p.m. September 14, 1980.

He's still missing and his case is classified as unsolved.

By this time, the fear in the African-American community was palpable. Although the task force was now offering a reward for the capture of the murderer, they were not close to solving the case. Conspiracy theories abound. Talk was resurrected that the killer was a member of the Ku Klux Klan or that there was a government cover up that protected the killer.

As a result, some activists in the community formed vigilante groups. One such group, called the bat patrol, sprang up in the Techwood Home housing project near Georgia Tech University. The members brandished baseball bats, thus their name.

In addition, concerned members of the community established genuine neighborhood watch groups. For the most part, African-American parents didn't allow their children out at night. If they had to go out, a grown up accompanied them.

Mayor Jackson announced a citywide curfew and in October the Atlanta City Council ordered Saturday searches. These events involved volunteers who searched wooded areas, vacant lots and dilapidated buildings for victims.

Then 10-year old Charles Stephens disappeared. Standing 5-feet tall and weighing 120 pounds, Charles lived with his mother, Ernestine Stephens, his father, Charles Stephens Sr., and his

sister Tina at 1707 Pryor Circle. He was a sixth-grade student at Perkerson Elementary School.

On Thursday, October 9, 1980, he left home to go to a friend or his cousin's home in Carver Homes, also known as the Villages at Carver.

His body was found the next day on a grassy hill near the entrance to Longview Trailer Park on Norman Berry Drive.

9-year old Aaron Jackson Jr. disappeared on Saturday, November 1, 1980. A student at Dobbs Elementary School, he lived with his father, Aaron Sr., two older sisters, Patricia, 16, and Lisa, 12, at 818 Norwood Road. He knew Aaron Wyche, a previous victim.

He was last seen at Moreland Avenue Shopping Center.

Aaron's body was found on the southeast bank of the South River off of Forest Park Road on November 2, 1980. Cause of death was asphyxiation by suffocation.

Patrick Rogers, a.k.a. "Pat Man", 16, was the 17th victim of the Atlanta Child Murders. He disappeared on Monday, November 10, 1980. A student at Grady High School, Patrick lived with his mother, Annie, three brothers and four sisters at the Thomasville Heights housing projects on Henry Thomas Drive SE. He enjoyed writing music with his friend Joe Harper. He also would help customers at the Moreland Avenue Shopping Center carry their groceries to their cars.

He was seen with his 7-year-old brother Isaac, at a bus stop on Henry Thomas Drive. A witness, Mary Harper, told police that he had come to her apartment at 1100 Henry Thomas Drive looking for her son, Joe Harper, and told her that a man wanted to record their songs. He was never seen alive again.

His body was found on December 7, 1980 on the Cobb County side of the Chattahoochee River near the Paces Ferry Road Bridge. He was the second of the murdered Atlanta children to be found in the Chattahoochee.

14-year old Lubie Geter was the next child to disappear. Called Chuck, he lived with his parents, a brother, and four sisters at 129 Dahlgren Street SE. A student at JC Murphy High School, he sold air fresheners at the National Pride Car Wash on Memorial Drive and also carried groceries for customers who shopped at a store nearby the car wash.

On Saturday, January 3, 1981, his brother drove him to the Big Star Food Store near Stewart-Lakewood Shopping Center on GA Route 6 where he sold car deodorizers.

A female witness later told police that she saw him getting into a car.

On the same day, a dog that was seen chasing rabbits in a wooded side of Vandiver Road near Enon Road found the body. A man who said that he was the killer called from a pay phone at Stewart Avenue nearby and tipped police.

When police arrived on the scene on February 5, 1981, they found Chuck wearing only white jockey shorts. His blue Levi's

and a brown belt was found about three-quarters of a mile away in a brown bag in a creek. His blue shirt and shoes were found about 300 yards away. Cause of death was manual strangulation.

Next was Terry Pue. 15-year-old Terry Lorenzo Pue lived in a housing project with his mother, Helen, and his father, Clarence at 2548 Hollywood Court NW.

A student at Challenge School at West Hunter Street Baptist Church, he knew Lubie "Chuck" Geter.

On Wednesday, January 22, 1981, he went to his neighbor Clinton Sewell's place to challenge him to a pick up basketball game. Clinton declined because it was raining. Terry replied that he would go ahead and shoot some hoops on his own.

He was seen later that night trading bottles for money near an A&P and Krystal Restaurant on Memorial Drive SE.

On January 23 a man walking in the area off Sigman Road in Rockdale County found the body and called police.

About two weeks before an anonymous man called police and told them that there was a boy's body at that location. When police went to the site, however, there was no body. The anonymous man called the police again and told them he placed a boy's body at the location. Again, when the police showed up, there was no body.

When police did discover Clinton's body, there were dog hairs on it as well as cuts on an elbow and bruises on the head.

Surgical scars on the child's right knee helped police identify the body. Cause of death was ligature strangulation.

Number 20 of the Atlanta murdered children was Patrick Baltazar. The 12-year-old lived at the Vine City Apartment on Foundry Street near the corner of Hynes, where the Georgia Dome, the stadium where the Atlanta Falcons play now stands. Patrick lived with his father Russell, his stepmother Sheila, and his brothers, Roger and Donald in a one-room apartment.

His father worked at the nearby Omni, where the Atlanta Flames of the National Hockey League and the Atlanta Hawks of the National Basketball Association played. It is now CNN Center, where the Cable News Network offices are located. He also worked at Fisherman's Cove.

Patrick would often go to the Galaxy Three Arcade to sell candy. A student at Bethune Elementary school, he also cleaned the Fisherman's Cove Restaurant, washed dishes at Papa's Country Buffet, and sold cotton candy at the Omni.

At about 4:30 p.m. on Friday, February 6, 1981, Patrick visited his father at the Fisherman's Cove to get money so he could attend a Golden Gloves Boxing Match at the Omni.

At about 2:00 p.m. February 13, 1981, a maintenance man for the Corporate Square Business Office Complex found Patrick's body in an overgrown area between the complex and apartments.

Police at the scene discovered scratches, bruises and dog hairs on the boy's body. Cause of death was ligature strangulation.

Curtis Lamar Walker III was the 21st victim. The 13-year-old boy was 5 feet tall and weighed just 75 pounds. He lived with his mother, Catherine Leach, two brothers, William and Alexander, and two sisters, Teaka and Kelclo Walker, in the Bowen Homes Apartments on Wilkes Circle NW. He was a 7th-grade student at the A.D. Williams School in Bowen Homes. He and one of his brothers would often go to the Byron Gun Shop on Bankhead Highway where they were paid for picking up trash outside the store.

On the day he disappeared on Thursday, February 19, 1981, he was seen at the gun shop looking for work. He was then seen walking to a nearby shopping center near the intersection of Bankhead Highway and Hightower Road.

As a fireman was crossing the South River at Waldrop Road near Flat Shoals Parkway, he found Curtis's body in the river caught on a log on March 6, 1981. He was wearing only underwear. Cause of death was strangulation.

A witness told police that he saw a green Chevy parked nearby the scene on Tuesday or Wednesday of the week before.

15-year-old Joseph "Jo Jo" Bell disappeared on Monday, March 2, 1981. A student at Booker T. Washington High School, He lived with his grandmother on Lawton Street SW. His mother Doris was in prison for killing the boy's father.

He often went to the John Harland Boys' Club on People's Street and the Dunbar Community Center and he worked at Cap'n Peg's Seafood.

An employee at Cap'n Peg's told police that she last saw Jo Jo playing basketball at Agnes Jones School. Jo Jo's friend Eugene Laster, 21, confirmed that the boy was playing basketball with him. He added that after the game he saw Jo Jo get into a station wagon on Westview Drive.

Two bikers riding on a new trail off of Klondike Road near the South River discovered Jo Jo's body on April 19, 1981. Police had to walk through woods for two miles to reach the site.

Jo Jo was wearing only underwear. Cause of death was asphyxiation.

Timothy Hill lived at 978 Sells Avenue SW with his mother Annie, his sisters, Mary and Brenda, and his brothers, Marion and Richard, who was a maintenance man at Thomasville Heights.

Richard knew Patrick "Pat Man" Rogers. Tim knew Jo Jo Bell, Patrick Baltazar, Anthony Carter and perhaps Alfred Evans, and Jeffery Mathis, who were all killed during the Atlanta Child Murder spree.

On Wednesday, March 11, 1981, Timothy was playing in his backyard with his niece. The niece said that she saw him get into a taxi with a man who put "mud" on his face.

A witness named Frankie Mealing, 34, claimed to have had consensual sex with Timothy at a house owned by Thomas Terrell at 530 Gray Street on Thursday at 5 p.m.

Terrell's neighbor claimed that Terrell kept a bucket of a drug the resembled mud and that people sniffed it to get high.

Mealing said that he then went to the house next door where Terrell lived. He added that at 9 p.m., Timothy came over and asked if he could stay the night because the last bus had left. Terrell agreed. Timothy stayed at Terrell's house that night.

The next day, Friday, March 13, he was seen standing on the sidewalk talking to a girl.

On Sunday, March 15, he was seen attending a rally for missing and murdered children at Morehouse College.

Timothy's teacher, Theresa Swindall, claimed that she received two phone calls from him on Monday March 16.

On March 30, 1981, two men fishing from canoes found Timothy Hill's body in the Chattahoochee River about a mile south of the Campbelton Road – GA Route 166 Bridge. He was wearing only underwear. The cause of death was asphyxiation.

Eddie "Bubba" Duncan Jr. was next. One of only a few adults to disappear and to be categorized as an Atlanta Child Murders victim, he was 21 years old and lived with his mother, Betty in an apartment on Hunnicutt Street NW in Techwood, a public housing project. A friend of Patrick "Pat Man" Rogers, Bubba worked at a small grocery store on the outskirts of the

Techwood Public Housing Project. He also did odd jobs at a nearby barbershop and at Courtney's Games and Things, next

door to the barbershop. He had spent one year in prison for having stolen goods.

On the day he disappeared on Friday, March 20, 1981, he boarded a MARTA bus at 2 p.m. with the intention of dropping clothes belonging to Calvin Coleman at a dry cleaning store and then meeting Coleman at Courtney's Games and Things.

The dry cleaning store records, however, showed that he didn't drop off the clothes until about 6 p.m. and he never showed up for his meeting with Coleman. He did not meet with his girlfriend Racine Clements that day as promised.

Earl Mallory, who knew Bubba because they both frequented Courtney's told police that he last saw him at about 7 p.m. walking back toward his apartment.

Other witnesses told police that they saw him at Courtney's and others said they saw him getting into a car near Courtney's.

On March 31, 1981, Canoeists paddling down the Chattahoochee River found Eddie Duncan's body in the water on the Douglas County side of the river near the GA Route 166

Bridge a few feet from where Timothy Hill's body was found the day before. He was wearing his boxers. Cause of death was undetermined.

Another adult, Larry Rogers, 20, disappeared on March 30 or April 1. He lived with his foster father, George Hood, at 1585 Ezra Church Drive NW.

One witness claimed seeing him at the intersection of Simpson Road NW and W. Lake Avenue NW on April 1, 1981. Another witness claimed that he saw him getting into a green Chevrolet station wagon with a light skinned man the afternoon of Monday, March 30.

Police found Larry's body in an apartment in a block of abandoned buildings on Temple Street on April 9. Dog hairs were present on the body and he was fully clothed. The cause of death was strangulation.

The third-consecutive adult who was categorized as a victim of the Atlanta Child Murders and found in the Chattahoochee River was Michael McIntosh a.k.a. Ricky Davis a.k.a. Michael Matthews a.k.a Mickey Williams. Not a big man, McIntosh was only 5-feet 3-inches tall and weighed only 116 pounds. He lived in a house he had inherited from his adoptive mother, Bessie McIntosh at 620 Windsor Street.

He worked odd jobs at Cap'n Peg's. The back of the building was directly across the street from his home. He also worked for Add-A-Man Labor Pool located on Spring Street NW and the Milton Avenue Foundry. He was a friend of Atlanta Child Murder victim Jo Jo Bell and the two often boxed together.

He was in prison at the Clark County Correctional Institution for burglary, armed robbery, possession of marijuana and attempted rape and also served in Reidsville and Putnam

County Prisons from 1976 to 1979 for receiving stolen property.

On March 24, 1981, he left his job at the Foundry and never returned.

The next day, March 25, a man who managed an import shop on Bankhead Highway (also known as US Route 278) told police that McIntosh, looking like he had been beaten badly, came into the shop seeking help. The manager gave him $12 and showed him where the nearest MARTA station was located and he saw him heading towards the Chattahoochee River.

On April 20, 1981, a Fulton County farmer named Jimmy Brown found his body on the bank of the River below the Cambellton Road Bridge near where the bodies of Timothy Hill and Eddie Duncan had been found. The body was naked. The cause of death was asphyxiation.

Jimmy Payne was the 27th victim and he too was found in the Chattahoochee River.

21 years old, Payne had been released from the Alto Correctional Institute in December 1980. He was in prison for burglary.

He lived at the Vine City Terrace Apartments on Magnolia Street NW with his sister, Evelyn, and his stepfather, Ula Jones.

He had attempted suicide at least twice and was under the care of a doctor.

He left home at 10:30 a.m. on either Tuesday, April 21 or Wednesday, April 22 to sell some 1951 nickels at the Omni and

to meet his girlfriend, Catherine Turner at the Vine City MARTA station later in the afternoon.

On April 27, 1981, Jesse Arnold and his wife were fishing on the east bank of the Chattahoochee River a mile north of the Bankhead Highway Bridge when they saw Payne's body. He was wearing only underwear.

The cause of death was asphyxiation.

Although the next victim was 17 years old, he already had a criminal record. William "Billy Star" Barrett had been arrested for aggravated assault, drug violations, theft, and receiving stolen property and had spent time in the Georgia Department of Offender Rehabilitation. He was also confined in a youth development center in Milledgeville, Georgia.

He lived in a house on 2nd Avenue NE. and it was said that he knew Lubie Geter, one of the victims.

William was last seen at the McDaniel-Glenn Housing Community Center paying a bill for his mother. A neighbor told police that she had seen him later a few blocks from his home in the Kirkwood-East Lake area along Memorial Drive getting into a two door white car with a black man at about 6 p.m. on Monday, May 11, 1981.

Some days later, an elementary school student claimed that someone had offered him $3,000 to kill William.

On May 12, 1981, FBI agents found his body on a curb in a wooded area on Winthrop Drive near Interstate 20 and Glenwood.

White undercoat animal hairs were found on the body. He was clothed, but missing a faded blue jean jacket. Also found on the body were an East Lake Meadows Boys Club card, two Willie Johnson Paint Company business cards, a Boy Scout pocket knife, and a piece of paper with the phone number traced back to a white man who had been seen at the Omni and the 5-Points MARTA Station trying to pick up boys. Another witness told police that they saw William at the man's house about one week before he disappeared. The witness also claimed to have seen Lubie "Chuck" Geter at the same house before his murder.

Cause of death was strangulation.

CHAPTER NINE

As bodies of murdered children turned up in different areas of metropolitan Atlanta, the Atlanta Police, Georgia Bureau of Investigation, and the FBI steadfastly kept on pace in their investigation to identify and arrest the killer.

The murders were having a national impact. President Ronald Reagan had sent Vice President George H. W. Bush to Atlanta to be briefed on the murders and the Reagan Administration contributed more than $2 million to find leads and to finance afterschool youth programs.

The FBI lab had identified the style of fabric of the fiber found on Eric Middlebrooks' shoe. The Bureau then sent letters to all carpet manufacturers in the United States to ask if they used this particular fabric in the manufacturing of their carpet. All but one manufacturer informed the FBI that they did not use that particular fabric. One company, the Wellman Company, located in South Carolina, notified the Bureau that they did manufacture carpet using that particular fabric.

The carpet was extremely unique. The Wellman Company enhanced a fabric used by another carpet manufacturer into a trilobal carpet that was more durable than the one they were improving.

Trilobal fibers feature three distinct sides. When light strikes the fiber it reflects back in a direct path resulting in a high-sheen appearance.

The Wellman Company created a trilobal fiber that had one short leg and two long legs, but it was very difficult to make. So the company produced a very small quantity thus making the carpet quite rare.

Once they had identified the fiber and its manufacturer, the FBI discovered that West Point Pepperell Company in Georgia bought the carpet from Wellman. They dyed their batch of carpets into 16 different colors. The dye called "English Olive" was used in just one-sixteenth of all the carpets sold by West Point Pepperell.

Another fiber found on 21 of the victims was made of unusual violet acetate.

Many more of the victims also had fibers used in carpets made for automobile manufacturers Plymouth, Ford, and Chevrolet.

The FBI also called on the skills and expertise of John E. Douglas. He created profiles on three of the most malicious serial killers David Berkowitz, Charles Manson, and Ted Bundy.

He guessed that the killer was an African-American male. It made sense, he would have been welcomed into the community and the victims would have been more inclined to trust him.

He also surmised that some of the evidence showed that the killer was a repressed homosexual.

Douglas also thought that the killer was smart and arrogate, an only child, and that his parents indulged him.

In addition, he thought that the killer would be a police buff, a small man in size and fairly light in weight. This was because most of the children that were murdered were small in size and light in weight. This would assure that the killer would be able to dominate them.

In May 1981, Douglas added one more trait. He believed that the killer would drop his victims in rivers in the Atlanta metropolitan area.

As a result of the prediction that the killer would dump bodies into Atlanta area rivers, the Atlanta police assigned officers to surveil close to a dozen area bridges including those that crossed the Chattahoochee River.

On May 22, 1981, a police officer on a bridge above the river heard a splash and notified police in the vicinity.

Another officer spotted a white 1970 Chevrolet station wagon make a U-turn and drive back across the bridge. Officers stopped the car about a half-mile from the bridge.

Driving the car was 23-year-old Wayne Bertram Williams, a music producer and freelance photographer. He told police that the car belonged to his parents.

Police ordered Williams out of the car, examined it, and found dog hairs, carpet fibers, gloves, and a 24-inch nylon cord.

During an interrogation, Williams said that he was traveling to the home of a woman named Cheryl Johnson, a singer, to audition her.

When the police asked where the woman lived, Williams responded Smyrna, a suburb of Atlanta.

After investigating the car, retrieving the dog hairs and carpet fibers, and a short interrogation, police let Williams climb back into his car and drive away.

Two days later, on May 24, 1981, two boys fishing in the Chattahoochee River about one half mile south of the I-285 bridge near

South Cobb Drive, between Jackson Parkway and Gordon Street spotted the nude body of Nathaniel Cater.

27-years old, Cater was living in the Falcon Hotel on Luckie Street NW. He had moved from his father's apartment on Verbena Street NW on April 24.

He worked for Add-A-Man Labor Pool and offered himself for sex at the Silver Dollar Saloon and Cameo Lounge on Spring Street.

At about 9:30 p.m. on Thursday, May 21, 1981, a gardener named Robert Henry saw Cater outside the Rialto Theatre on Forsyth Street NW holding hands with Wayne Williams.

Police believed that it was Cater's body that caused the splash that they heard and that Wayne Williams had thrown him off the bridge before his encounter with police.

The police learned during their investigation that a number of people who were last to see victims before they disappeared, said they saw them with Williams. Family members of other victims said that they knew Williams and that he had come to their home.

Others in the African-American community, including children who were friends of victims, told police that Williams handed out flyers that invited young people between the ages of 11 and 21 to audition for his new boys' band he called Gemini. The mother of Randy Joe Heath, the last person to see Alfred Evans, the second victim of the Atlanta Child Murders, told police that she knew Wayne Williams and had suggested that he pass out his flyers at Thomasville Heights where Aaron Wyche and Patrick Rogers lived. Wyche was victim 10 and Patrick Rogers was victim 17. She said that Williams told her later that he had found a young man at

Moreland Avenue Shopping Center who he hired to distribute the handouts.

CHAPTER TEN

Wayne Williams was now the prime suspect. He was asked to come down to police headquarters in downtown Atlanta to take polygraph tests. He failed all of them.

Next, the police obtained a warrant to search Williams' parents' home where the suspect lived. What they found was a treasure trove of evidence.

First, the carpet that covered the floor of the entire house was English Olive, the same carpet that the Wellman Company of South Carolina had manufactured and that the West Point Pepperell Company bought from Wellman. Seventeen victims were found with at least one fiber of the carpet on them.

Unusual violet acetate fibers that were interwoven with green cotton were found on 21 victims. Police found a bedspread in William's bedroom that was made of the same violet acetate and green cotton.

Police found a yellow blanket under Williams' bed that matched fibers found on six victims.

Williams also had a German Shepard. Police took samples of her hair and found that they matched with dog hair found on 20 victims.

During the murder spree Williams had owned or driven a variety of cars including a decommissioned Plymouth detective's car, a red Ford LTD, and a Chevrolet station wagon.

Fibers on many of the victims matched carpet from those cars at times when Williams was known to have driven them.

In addition, police discovered the alleged weapon that was used to kill many of the victims — a slapjack also known as a blackjack. It is similar to a police baton that features reinforced steel covered with leather and also includes a hand strap and slapper area. Police found it hidden in a ceiling panel above Williams' office at his home.

Moreover, John Douglas' profile fit Williams' characteristics. He had guessed that the killer had promise, but never reached his potential. He also guessed that the killer's parents treated him as a gifted child and yet he dropped out of school. He couldn't hold a steady job and life was not going well.

Douglas' profile also concluded that the killer's parents had idolized him. He also guessed that the killer was a police aficionado who was articulate and who followed the crime.

Born on May 27, 1958, Williams was brought up in the Dixie Hills section of southwest Atlanta. His parents, Homer and Faye Williams, were teachers.

He was an "A" student in school and all the teachers who taught him were greatly impressed with his demeanor and intelligence. He was quiet and respectful.

Still, Williams was a loner and considered a nerd by many of his classmates. His serious demeanor compounded by the fact that he wore glasses made him the favorite target of bullies.

Williams, however, was able to avoid violent confrontations due to his wit and learned how to manipulate people when the need arose.

Williams graduated at the top of his class from Douglass High School where he had served as student council president. He learned how to disassemble and re-assemble radios. He became so competent at it that he actually fixed the radios of friends and family for free. He repaired radios for others for a price.

He actually built his own radio station and often visited stations in the area including WIGO and WAOK. He built friendships with several of the announcers of both stations and actually worked at them part time.

He applied and was accepted to some of the local universities and even received some scholarships. Except for short stint at Georgia State University, however, where he took business and finance courses, he considered himself a potential entrepreneur who didn't need a college education.

He pursued a career as a music producer and manager. He was a fan of rhythm and blues and enjoyed Motown and soul music. So, it shouldn't be surprising that his favorite group throughout the 1970s was the Jackson Five.

Like most, Williams loved music, but he didn't have the natural talent to pursue a singing career of his own.

He worked to create contacts with people who were involved in the music scene in Atlanta. He would drop the names of some of these people when talking to kids when convincing them that he was creating a boys' band like the Jackson 5 that he called Gemini. He actually auditioned kids at a local Atlanta studio where they made demo tapes.

Williams promoted his desire to create a boys' band through word of mouth and flyers that he distributed at locations that young black teens would hang out.

At night he pursued a career as a freelance photographer who often visited crime scenes to take pictures. He used a police scanner to learn the location of the crime scenes.

He'd prowl the streets of Atlanta at night driving his car and listening to a police scanner and band radio waiting for a report that would provide an address of where there was a fire, accident and a crime scene. He would then pounce onto the scene, take photographs and then return home where he developed the film.

He also had a reputation for stretching the truth or telling outright lies. For example, he claimed to be a national honor student and bragged that he was in the junior ROTC when in high school. He was arrested once for impersonating a police officer and boasted to some that he was a fighter pilot or an agent of the Central Intelligence Agency.

After the home was searched, there was no announcement or indication that Williams' arrest was imminent. The police figured he did it, but they wanted to make certain that they had an airtight case. So, while police worked to finalize the case, Williams decided to hold a press conference. He knew that the search of his parents' home didn't look good for him and the community was already talking about and watching him. He wanted to use the press conference as a way to claim his innocence.

The day after the search, he contacted the major media outlets of the city to invite them to his parents' home. He agreed that the meeting could be on camera, but he specified that his face not be shown.

Early in the press conference Williams was asked about the victims.

"Some of these kids go to places they have no business being at certain times in the day or night," he responded. "Some of them don't have no home supervision and they're running around the streets wild. I'm saying that when you're doing that, that's not giving anyone a license to kill, but you're opening yourself up for all kinds of things."

Williams claimed that the Task Force was out to get him. He backed that up saying, "One of the Task Force captains pointed his finger at me and said he was tired of all the BS about working long hours, working the stakeouts and he was ready to pull things to an end."

He concluded the press conference saying, "I'm asking for a public apology by the FBI or whoever was responsible for leaking information about me to the news media."

Whether he expected it or not, he gained even more notoriety as a result of the press conference. The media published the address of his parents' home and exhibited all sorts of photographs of him. The worldwide media identified him as the prime suspect in the Atlanta Child Murders.

The media and Task Force hounded Williams for a consecutive 17 days after the press conference.

The Task Force placed a tracking device on his white station wagon.

Regular citizens, the police, and members of the Task Force camped outside his home. Williams said that he would sue the media and Task Force for harassment.

Sometimes, late at night, he would leave his home, get into his white station wagon and drive. Some members of the Task

Force feared that he would be searching for another victim. But most in the Task Force hoped that was the case so that they could catch him during the act.

The Task Force finalized their case and Williams was arrested on June 21, 1981. He was charged for the murders of Nathaniel Cater and Jimmy Payne. Prosecutors categorized 10 of the murders as "pattern cases" and used them in the trial to prove that Williams followed a specific pattern when committing the murders.

The "pattern cases" included the murders of Alfred Evans, Eric Middlebrooks, Charles Stephens, Lubie Geter, Terry Pue, Patrick Baltazar, Joseph Bell, Larry Rogers, William Barrett, and John Porter.

CHAPTER ELEVEN

Once Wayne Williams was arrested and charged for only two of the murders, many in the media and the Atlanta community questioned why more murders were not charged to him.

Serial killer cases are complicated. Prosecutors want to make their case as airtight as possible. So, in this case, they preferred to try Williams only on the murders of Nathaniel Cater and Jimmy Payne because they believed the evidence in these cases were best for convicting him.

To back up the two murders for which Williams was charged, the prosecution focused on 10 other cases to show that Williams was connected and to establish a pattern. Prosecutors believed that they could have charged Williams for as many as 15 to 18 murders. But such a large amount of cases in one trial could prove too difficult for a jury to follow.

In addition, five of the murders occurred outside Fulton County and thus was outside the jurisdiction of the prosecution. Still, some of these cases were tied to the 10 Williams was not prosecuted for to prove a pattern.

When it became clear to the Task Force that Williams was their only suspect, the Fulton County's Sheriff's Office built an additional wing on to the jail only to house Williams. The wing was constructed to serve as a deterrent against Williams somehow escaping as well as to keep other inmates of the Fulton County Jail from killing him.

Rumors were flying that people who may have wanted Williams dead had made it known in the prison community that they wanted the job done.

The Sheriff's Office didn't want to be thought of as responsible for Williams' death because it could have led to a whole new set of conspiracy theories.

When Williams was arrested on June 21, 1981, he was, for all intent and purposes held in solitary confinement. He was under 24-hours observation to prevent any suicide attempt. Only his lawyers were allowed in.

The time between Williams' arrest and the the trial allowed his attorneys to develop a case. But it also allowed public attention on the trial to grow. Reporters from just about every media outlet in the United States as well as some from outside the country came to Atlanta to cover the event. It actually became one of the first serial murder cases to experience so much media scrutiny.

It was believed by many who followed the case that Williams' attorneys would present a pre-trial motion to change the venue of the trial. Williams' attorneys, however, did not request a change of location. They believed that he could get a fair trial because the jury would consist of people who lived in his hometown and that a majority of the jury would be African American. His attorneys' believed that he had a better chance for a fair review in Atlanta then in any other region of Georgia where there were fewer blacks.

As far as the jury was concerned, the prosecution didn't want to appear racist. They didn't worry that a predominately African-American jury could convict him. After all, the victims were all African American. In the end, the jury consisted of eight African Americans and four whites. The breakdown in terms of gender was nine women and three men.

To avoid any impression of bias toward either side, a computer selected the judge who would preside over the trial. The person selected was Clarence Cooper, the first black judge to be elected to the bench in Fulton County.

The trial began on January 6, 1982. The prosecution, led by Jack Mallard, started the trial relying on the testimony of FBI profilers. The profile in the Atlanta Child Murder case did not only describe the characteristics of the killer. It also included profiles of the victims.

The profilers who testified noted that all the victims were African American, most were male, and all were younger than 30.

They noted that most serial killers murder people of their own race. They also pointed out, however, that Williams had a hatred of blacks. They proved Williams' hatred toward the race based on what he had said in the past and based on the fact that the killings were committed "hands on."

They also compared the profile of the suspected killer to Williams and noted that the killer was black, that he had great potential and yet let all of that slip away. He had dropped out of school, was very smart, and couldn't hold a job, an only child that his parents idolized, a police buff who followed crimes, and was articulate.

They also noted that the fact he was a music producer or talent manager who was trying to create an all-boys' band similar to the Jackson 5 gave him access to black male children. Moreover, the fact that he was black would allow him to get close to potential victims that would not be possible if the killer were white.

The profilers also pointed out that there was a sexual context to the murders. Although there was no semen found on the bodies, there was a sexual component in the fact that the killer acted on his sexual frustration. And, the fact that many of the bodies were nude when discovered showed that the killer was sexually aroused by the activity.

But most of the case against Williams was based on the forensic evidence and the eyewitnesses.

A group of attorneys who were appointed by the court provided Williams' defense. The lead attorney was Mary

Welcome. She was known in the legal profession of Atlanta and had served as a city solicitor. It was her first murder case, however, and, as the trial proceeded, it was evident that the prosecution outmatched her.

Welcome chose Tony Axam, who had more trial experience than she did to assist. But before the trial started, Williams fired him and appointed another attorney named Alvin Binder. He was from Mississippi and was known in the legal trade as confrontational. He aggressively questioned witnesses in a manner that didn't help the defense's presentation.

Welcome and Binder did not present any expert witnesses to challenge the fiber evidence nor did they present some alternative scenario to explain the crimes. Instead, they concentrated on the fact that none of this evidence was 100 percent certain. They also challenged the witnesses.

They argued that Williams didn't kill anyone, that he was at the wrong place at the wrong time, and that the witnesses were mistaken when they linked Williams to the crimes.

Wayne Williams himself was the major witness for the defense. He was adamant about testifying.

Williams was on the stand for three days. On the first two days he did fairly well because Welcome and Binder were questioning him. He wasn't challenged. He kept his composure, was polite, and appeared timid and passive.

But on the third day of his testimony, the prosecution challenged him and he became frustrated. At one point, he was so angry that he shot back to the prosecutor, "Do you want the real Wayne Williams? You got him!"

He later called the prosecutor a "dropshot," meaning that he was unworthy in the urban vernacular of African Americans. An earlier witness testified that Williams used the term when referring to the murdered children.

Each question that the prosecution shot out toward Williams made him even angrier. Williams became more combative with his answers.

When Mallard asked him about the testimony of Robert Henry, who said that he saw Cater outside the Rialto Theatre on Forsyth Street NW holding hands with Wayne Williams the night that Cater disappeared, Williams responded, "I done told you I don't hold hands with no man no where."

Williams explained some years later that his attorneys told him to be more combative with the prosecution. They thought he had been too timid the first day of his testimony. He also said that he regretted taking the stand in the trial.

Williams' defense to this day is that no one actually saw him kill anyone.

After deliberating for 12 hours, on February 27, 1982 the jury found Wayne Williams guilty of two counts of first-degree murder.

CHAPTER TWELVE

While Wayne Williams serves his life term in Hancock State Prison in Georgia, many in Atlanta believe that he did not commit any of the murders, but most believe that he committed some, if not most of them.

Many still favor one of many conspiracy theories to support their opinions. These theories blame the Ku Klux Klan, the Atlanta Police Department, the FBI, a gang of pedophiles, and on and on.

Those who have taken the time to examine the case between the verdict and now reason that the murders of some of the victims didn't fit Williams' so-called MO. Even members of the task force had their doubts. In addition, the Atlanta Police announced just prior to Williams' arrest that the killer had an accomplice. There were many in the Task Force who supported that.

Many more asserted that Williams did kill many of the victims, but not all.

The lead prosecutor in the case, Jack Mallard, asserted some time after the trial that he thinks he could have convicted Williams of 15 to 20 of the murders.

One of the profilers in the case, John E. Douglas, noted in his book *Mindhunter* that Williams had killed 11 of the Atlanta Child Murder victims. He added that the evidence didn't connect him to "all or even most of the deaths and disappearances of children …"

Most have doubts that Williams had killed the two girls – Latonya Wilson and Angel Lenair. Their murders did not follow his pattern.

Wilson had been abducted from her home. The only element of the crime that did match Williams' MO was that her body was found in a vacant lot.

Moreover, the murders of which Williams was convicted as well as the ones used to serve as pattern cases in the trial indicate that he was a repressed homosexual. Such a suspect would not have murdered two little girls.

The pattern of the cases in which Williams was convicted and were used to support those murders was that he attracted the victims with hopes of being a member of his boys' band or that he had made a sexual overture to get the victim into his car.

Even the murder of Eric Middlebrooks, which was the first to bring attention to the carpet fiber evidence didn't follow

Williams' regular pattern of cause of death and the location in which the body was found.

While Williams' pattern was to strangle or asphyxiate the victim, Middlebrooks, was beaten to death. The only element of this crime that fit Williams' MO. was that the victim was killed in one location and dumped in another.

The question of whether Williams had an accomplice is an intriguing one. Although some of the evidence may imply that, the prospect doesn't fit with the fact that he was a loner.

Still, it is the conspiracy theories that grabs on to many. One theory that the task force thought was serious enough to investigate surmise that a pedophile ring was involved with the murders.

According to the theory, many of the African-American elite of Atlanta including prominent businessmen and politicians were compensating young men who were involved in petty crimes to kidnap black children, deliver them to the community elite to be sexually abused and then they were killed and dumped by the men who had abducted them.

The case of Michael McIntosh seemed to give some element of the pedophile theory credence. McIntosh had a criminal record and he associated with some shady characters. He used drugs and offered himself for sex.

A tipster told police that people who had hired him for sex may have killed him.

The task force followed up on the tip but couldn't find any evidence that proved it.

In addition, when investigating the deaths of victims Patrick Baltazar, JoJo Bell, and Timothy Hill, the police discovered that all three boys knew Larry Marshal, who was not only a petty criminal who sold drugs, burglarized homes, and robbed stores, he was also a pimp who was said to have managed a brothel where the three boys were known to have worked at various times.

At the time the police discovered this, Marshal was in the Hartford, Connecticut jail waiting to be tried on felony counts. He was also wanted for a stabbing and robbery in Atlanta.

The Task Force interviewed him in Connecticut concerning his connection to the three boys, but they determined that he had not killed them.

Perhaps why the Ku Klux Klan conspiracy gained some traction is because many people claimed to have heard Charles T. Sanders making comments about the victims and about the murders in general. Sanders was a known white supremacist and a member of the Klan. A statement he made praising the murders was secretly taped.

Some time after the trial he supposedly said that he was lucky that he and Williams had the same carpet and that they both owned a German Shepard dog.

Police checked him out and even gave him a polygraph test. He passed the test and police dropped him as a suspect.

A theory that many in the field of police work support is that some who made the list as being victims of the Atlanta Child Murders were actually killed by members of their own family.

A former member of the Task Force and Deputy Director of the Atlanta Criminal Investigation Unit, Mike Edward, believes that a family member killed some of the victims on the list.

CHAPTER THIRTEEN

Since his conviction Wayne Williams have initiated a number of appeals.

In the 1990s, he filed a *habeas corpus* petition and asked for a retrial. Butts County Superior Court Judge Hall Craig denied it.

In 2004, Williams again asked for a retrial arguing that the Atlanta Police covered up evidence that showed involvement of the Ku Klux Klan and that the carpet fiber evidence could not withstand scientific challenge. A federal judge rejected the request in 2006.

Due to advancements in DNA analysis, the FBI re-tested two human hairs found on one of the victims in 2007. The mitochondrial DNA sequence in the hairs would eliminate 98 percent of African Americans. The test did match Williams' DNA, however, thus not eliminating the possibility that the hair tested was his.

Also in 2007, the genetics laboratory at the University of California, Davis School of Veterinary Medicine tested dog hairs found on the body of Patrick Baltazar. They discovered that the DNA sequence was in the hair of William's German Shepherd. While calling the finding "significant,"

Elizabeth Wictum, the director of the lab, asserted that the test was not "conclusive," because the mitochondrial DNA could not show that the sample hair was unique to one dog. The hairs showed the same DNA sequence as Williams' dog., but the same sequence appears in about 1 in 100 dogs. So Williams' dog could not be excluded and, as a result, Williams remains as a suspect in the murder of Baltazar.

In 2019, Atlanta Mayor Keisha Lance Bottoms and Atlanta Police Chief Erika Shields announced that evidence from the Atlanta Child Murder Case would be re-tested using advanced DNA analysis that was not available when the murders occurred 40 years ago.

Although DNA analysis could be performed in the 1980s, it could only be used to match to type. Scientists could not read the specific DNA code of each individual.

So, a review of the case including more sophisticated DNA analysis may finally answer the question once and for all -- is Wayne Williams the Atlanta child murderer?

Murders that occur about 40 years ago are often forgotten. The Atlanta Child Murder Case has remained before the world due to movies, TV miniseries, and books.

The first of the television mini-series was *The Atlanta Child Murders*, shown on CBS in February 1985. Touted as a fictional portrayal of the actual events, the movie concludes that Williams is probably the killer, but he is not to blame for murdering many of the other victims on the task force list.

A movie broadcast in 2000 on Showtime called *Who Killed Atlanta's Children?* advocates the conspiracy theory that the Ku Klux Klan did it.

In 2010, CNN showed a documentary called, *The Atlanta Child Murders*. The show featured Soledad O'Brien interviews with people involved in the story including Wayne Williams. Viewers were encouraged to log on to CNN.com to cast votes on whether they thought Williams did or did not commit the murders or that the case wasn't proven. 68.6 percent of respondents voted that Williams had done it. Only 4.3 percent concluded that he was innocent.

In January 2018, a documentary film producer, Payne Lindsey, released a podcast dubbed *Atlanta Monster* that features interviews of Wayne Williams, family members of the victims, law enforcement personnel, and people who were alive in Atlanta at the time of the murders.

The most recent of the television depictions is the Netflix series *Mindhunter*. The murders was the focus of the show's second season.

Whether or not these television shows, movies and documentaries pressured Atlanta authorities to re-visit the Atlanta Child Murders that occurred between 1979 and 1981, the case is again open.

According to Mayor Keisha Lance Bottoms, the purpose of re-opening the case of the Atlanta Child Murders is not to vindicate the conviction of Wayne Williams, but to finally offer closure to the families of all the victims

Atlanta, Fulton County, and the Georgia Bureau of Investigation will study never-before scrutinized evidence as well as re-examine the other evidence of the case.

"We don't know what we'll find," said Atlanta Police Chief Erika Shields, "but the city feels an obligation to do everything it can to provide answers and will look through every box of evidence to see if something warrants closer analysis."